· ANIMALS ILLUSTRATED ·

Muskox

·ANIMALS ILLUSTRATED·
Muskox

by Allen Niptanatiak • illustrated by Kagan McLeod

INHABIT
MEDIA

Published by Inhabit Media Inc.
www.inhabitmedia.com

Inhabit Media Inc. (Iqaluit), P.O. Box 11125, Iqaluit, Nunavut, X0A 1H0 (Toronto), 191 Eglinton Avenue East, Suite 301, Toronto, Ontario, M4P 1K1

Editors: Neil Christopher, Kelly Ward
Art Director: Danny Christopher
Designer: Astrid Arijanto

We acknowledge the support of the Canada Council for the Arts for our publishing program.

This project was made possible in part by the Government of Canada.

ISBN: 978-1-77227-122-5

Printed in Canada

Library and Archives Canada Cataloguing in Publication

Niptanatiak, Allen, author
Muskox / by Allen Niptanatiak ; illustrated by Kagan McLeod.

(Animals illustrated)
ISBN 978-1-77227-122-5 (hardback)

I. Muskox--Juvenile literature.
I. McLeod, Kagan, illustrator II. Title. III. Series: Animals illustrated

QL737.U53N56 2016   j599.64'78   C2016-907368-8

Table of Contents

The Muskox

The muskox is a large, hoofed animal that lives in the Arctic. Muskoxen look a bit like buffalo or bison, but they have long shaggy hair, a humped back, and very large, curved horns. The hair of the muskox is usually very dark brown to black in colour, with a patch of white on the shoulders.

Male muskoxen are called "bulls" and female muskoxen are called "cows."

A bull muskox usually weighs about 595 to 695 pounds (270 to 315 kilograms), and a cow usually weighs about 396 to 496 pounds (180 to 225 kilograms). Both male and female muskoxen have horns.

Muskoxen like to live in large groups called "herds." A herd usually has about 10 to 25 muskoxen, but herds can have as many as 40 to 60 muskoxen in some areas.

Let's learn more about muskoxen!

Range

Muskoxen are found on the Arctic tundra. They are found in different areas of the tundra in the warmer and colder months. They stay in the Arctic all year long, but they have been known to travel about 60 to 100 miles (97 to 161 kilometres) in search of food.

In the summer months, muskoxen can be found in valleys, along river banks and lake shores, and in grassy meadows. During the winter, when the wind blows the snow away from hilltops and cliffs, muskoxen move to this higher ground because it is easier to find food.

Skeleton

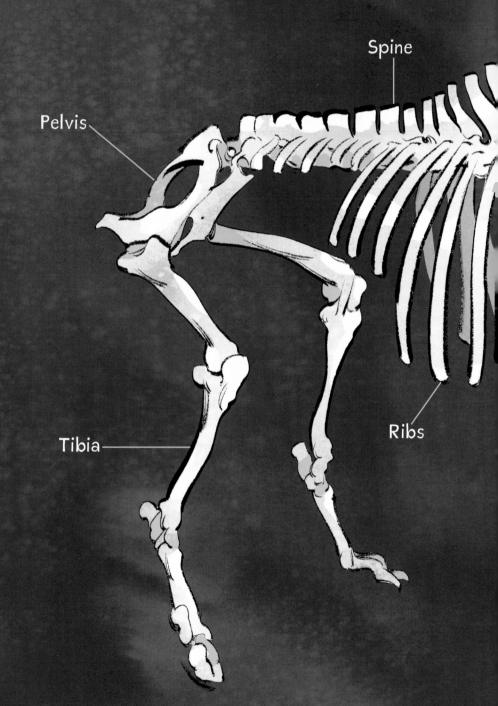

Spine

Pelvis

Ribs

Tibia

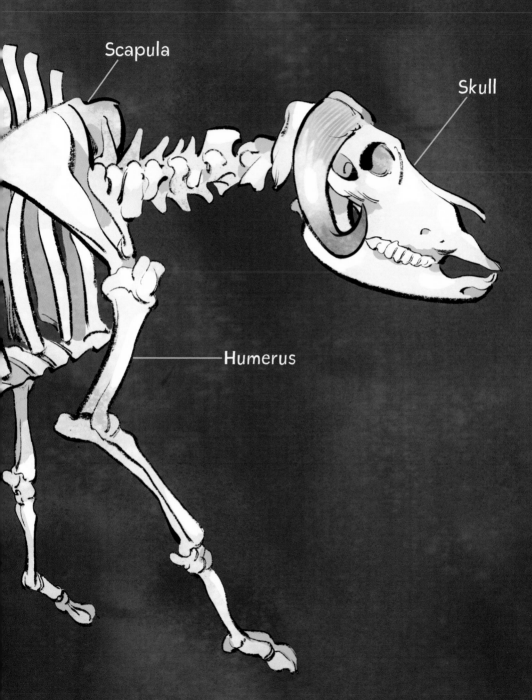

Scapula

Skull

Humerus

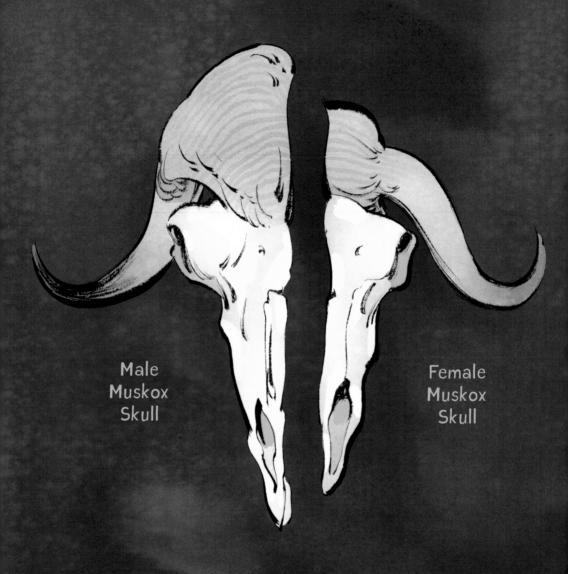

Male
Muskox
Skull

Female
Muskox
Skull

Both male and female muskoxen have curved horns that grow from the tops of their heads down to their jaw bones and then curve out into sharp points. The horns of the male muskox are much bigger than the female's, and the horns of the female are usually darker in colour.

Muskoxen use their hard hooves to help them find plants to eat.

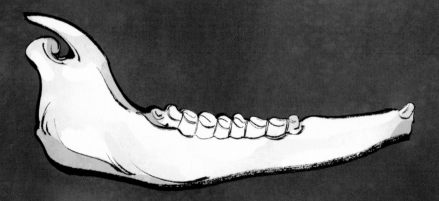

Muskox Jaw

Diet

Muskoxen are herbivores. That means they only eat plants. Muskoxen usually eat tundra grasses, Arctic willows, and leaves. During the summer, they can feed anywhere on the tundra where there are lots of grasses and willows growing.

Arctic Willow

Tundra Grass

During the winter, muskoxen eat the dried plants that can be found on hilltops. They use their hooves to dig up dried grasses and other plants from beneath the snow.

Babies

A baby muskox is called a "calf." Muskox cows have their calves in the early spring months of March and April. Usually only one calf is born, but very rarely a cow may have twins.

Cows usually move just a short distance away from the herd to have a baby, and will come right back to the herd as soon as the baby is able to walk well.

Muskox calves can walk well enough to keep up with the herd just a few hours after being born!

Predators

Even though they are very large and have sharp horns, there are animals in the Arctic that will try to catch and eat muskoxen. These animals are called "predators."

Wolves and grizzly bears are the main predators of muskoxen.

Wolves hunt in groups, attacking the muskoxen from many sides, so they are very dangerous to muskoxen—especially babies and young calves.

Defense

Muskoxen have a very special way of protecting themselves when predators come close. A herd of muskoxen will form a circle, or sometimes a tight line, with the adults facing the danger and the young animals inside the circle or behind the line for protection.

The largest bull will usually stand right in front of the predator, and may be a few paces ahead of the rest of the herd. The muskoxen are able to defend themselves because the sharp horns of the entire herd face the predator. When bears or wolves cannot break this circle, they will usually move away to look for an easier meal.

Withstanding the Cold

Winters in the Arctic can be very, very cold. Many places in the Arctic are too cold for some animals to stay there during the coldest months of winter. But muskoxen stay in the Arctic all year long.

In Kugluktuk, Nunavut, where there are lots of muskoxen, the temperature has dropped to -58 degrees Fahrenheit (-50 degrees Celsius). So how do muskoxen withstand this cold?

Muskoxen have special hair that helps them fight the cold. The hairs on the outside of a muskox's coat, known as "guard hairs," are long and shaggy. Underneath the guard hairs is another layer of fine, soft hair, called "undercoat." The undercoat traps heat to keep the muskox warm. In the summer months, when it is warmer, muskoxen lose their undercoat so that they don't overheat.

Fun Facts

All muskoxen use their
sharp horns to warn off
predators, but muskox
bulls also use them to fight
each other for the right to
be the lead bull of the herd
during the mating season.

Bulls will fight by charging each
other and butting heads. Bulls run
toward each other at a full gallop, and
the sound their heads make when they hit
is so loud it can be heard from miles away!

Bulls will also make loud roaring noises during
this time of year, to let other bulls know that
they are ready to fight.

Traditional Uses

Inuit have lived with and hunted muskoxen for thousands of years in the Arctic, and they have many uses for these animals.

Muskox skins are very warm and soft. Inuit traditionally used them as bedding inside iglus.

The undercoat that muskoxen lose in the spring—called *"qiviut"* in Inuktitut—was traditionally gathered from the tundra after it fell and was used to line mitts to make them extra warm.

Muskox meat is also eaten by Inuit across the Arctic.

Muskox Skin

Qiviut

Muskox Stew

Allen Niptanatiak is a hunter and trapper from Kugluktuk, Nunavut.

Kagan McLeod has been illustrating for magazines, newspapers, and design firms since 1999, after graduating from Sheridan College's illustration program. He began work as a staff artist for the *National Post* newspaper, and has had illustration work published recently in *Entertainment Weekly*, *Reader's Digest*, *The Walrus*, *The Wall Street Journal*, *Toronto Life*, *The Boston Globe*, and *Popular Mechanics*. His first graphic novel, *Infinite Kung-Fu*, was published in 2012. He lives in Toronto with his wife, two daughters, and a hound dog.